Read About
Amelia Earhart

Stephen Feinstein

Enslow Elementary

an imprint of

Enslow Publishers, Inc.

40 Industrial Road   PO Box 38
Box 398   Aldershot
Berkeley Heights, NJ 07922   Hants GU12 6BP
USA   UK

http://www.enslow.com

Words to Know

license (LIE-sense)—A card or paper showing that a person has permission to do something, such as drive or fly.

navigator (NAH-vih-gay-tur)—A person on a ship or plane who is in charge of finding the way to go.

pilot (PIE-lut)—Someone who flies a plane.

publish (PUB-lish)—To print a book.

stunt—A difficult act showing great skill or courage.

World War I—A war that lasted from 1914 to 1918 in Europe. The United States entered the war in 1917.

Enslow Elementary, an imprint of Enslow Publishers, Inc.

Enslow Elementary® is a registered trademark of Enslow Publishers, Inc.

Library of Congress Cataloging-in-Publication Data

Feinstein, Stephen.
    Read about Amelia Earhart / Stephen Feinstein.
        p. cm. — (I like biographies!)
    Includes bibliographical references and index.
    ISBN 0-7660-2582-9
    1. Earhart, Amelia, 1897–1937—Juvenile literature.
2. Air pilots—United States—Biography—Juvenile
literature. 3. Women air pilots—United States—
Biography—Juvenile literature. I. Title. II. Series.
    TL540.E3F45 2006
    629.13'092—dc22
    [B]
                                            2005009796

Printed in the United States of America

10 9 8 7 6 5 4 3 2 1

To Our Readers: We have done our best to make sure all Internet Addresses in this book were active and appropriate when we went to press. However, the author and the publisher have no control over and assume no liability for the material available on those Internet sites or on links to other Web sites. Any comments or suggestions can be sent by e-mail to comments@enslow.com or to the address on the back cover.

Every effort has been made to locate all copyright holders of material used in this book. If any errors or omissions have occurred, corrections will be made in future editions of this book.

Illustration Credits: All photos are from the Schlesinger Library, Radcliffe Institute for Advanced Study, Harvard University, except the following: Artville, LLC, p. 13 (bottom); Library of Congress, pp. 7, 13 (top), 19.

Cover Illustration: Library of Congress.

Contents

Amelia Earhart was born in Kansas on July 24, 1897. As a young girl, Amelia liked to do things that other girls did not. She played baseball and football with the boys. She liked to climb over fences. While the other girls stayed inside, Amelia played outside.

These are some of Amelia's family pictures.

Amelia's parents

Amelia as a baby

Amelia with Muriel, her
little sister

Amelia, age 6

Amelia loved to look at maps and to read about faraway places. She dreamed about taking trips to all of those places.

When Amelia was eleven, her father took her to the Iowa State Fair. There Amelia saw a strange-looking thing fly through the air. Her father told her it was an airplane.

This plane is probably like the one Amelia saw. To her it looked like a box kite made of wood and rusty wire.

During **World War I**, Amelia helped take care of wounded **pilots** in a hospital in Canada. The pilots told her a lot about flying. Amelia visited nearby airfields. She learned how airplanes worked. She watched pilots do **stunts** in the air. For the first time, Amelia wanted to fly.

Here is Amelia dressed for nursing. During World War I, she met many pilots.

9

In the summer of 1920, Amelia went to an air show in California with her father. There she took her first airplane ride. As soon as the airplane left the ground, Amelia knew she wanted to learn to fly.

In 1921, Amelia took her first flying lesson. The next year, she got her pilot's **license**. She began flying planes in her spare time.

Amelia's first flying teacher was Neta Snook (on the left). To earn money to pay for flying, Amelia taught English to children from other countries.

Chapter 3

Amelia Flies Across the Atlantic Ocean

In June 1927, Charles Lindbergh was the first person to fly a plane alone across the Atlantic Ocean. The next year, Amelia became the first woman to travel by air across the Atlantic. Wilmer Stultz and Lou Gordon flew the *Friendship* while Amelia checked the maps. The flight from Canada to Wales took twenty hours and forty minutes.

Here are Wilmer Stutz, Amelia Earhart, and Lou Gordon after their flight across the Atlantic Ocean. The map shows the path taken by their plane, the *Friendship*.

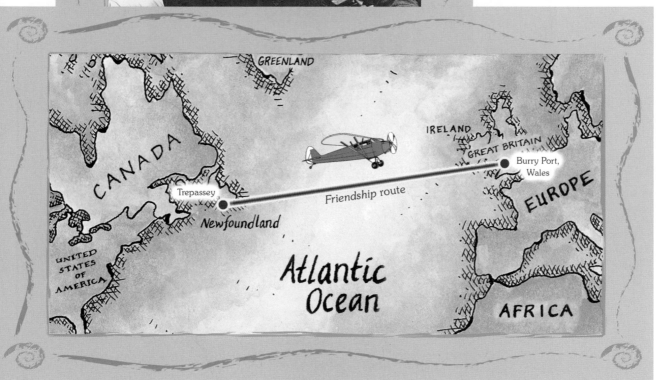

Amelia was now famous. She wrote a book about the flight. She traveled all around the country, giving speeches about women and flying. At that time, women did not do many of the jobs that men did. Amelia believed that women should be free to choose the same jobs as men.

Amelia Earhart did many things that few women did at that time. Here she is putting her plane in position before takeoff.

In 1931, Amelia married George Putnam. He had **published** one of her books. The next year, Amelia became the first woman to fly an airplane alone across the Atlantic. The flight from Canada to Ireland took over fourteen hours. President Herbert Hoover gave Amelia a gold medal.

In this picture, George Putnam is helping Amelia put on her parachute before a flight.

Chapter 4

Amelia's Last Plane Flight

Amelia became the first person to fly alone from Hawaii to California in 1935. She then started to plan her greatest adventure yet. Amelia wanted to become the first woman to fly around the world.

In May 1937, Amelia and her **navigator**, Fred Noonan, took off from California and flew east, stopping in South America, Africa, and Asia.

Fred Noonan and Amelia Earhart check the plane before takeoff. They flew to many of the places Amelia had dreamed about when she was younger.

On July 2, Amelia and Fred took off from the country of New Guinea, heading for tiny Howland Island in the Pacific Ocean. Sadly, they never got there. They disappeared, and their airplane was never found.

We will always remember Amelia Earhart for her flying skills and her great courage.

Amelia Earhart showed women that they could do the kinds of things men have done, no matter how difficult.

Timeline

1897—Amelia is born in Kansas on July 24.

1920—Amelia takes her first airplane ride.

1921—Amelia takes her first flying lesson.

1922—Amelia gets her pilot's license.

1928—Amelia becomes the first woman to fly across the Atlantic Ocean.

1931—Amelia marries George Putnam.

1932—Amelia becomes the first woman to fly alone across the Atlantic Ocean.

1934—Amelia becomes the first person to fly alone from Hawaii to California.

1937—Amelia's plane disappears on July 2, during the last part of her flight around the world.

Learn More

Books

Adler, David A. *A Picture Book of Amelia Earhart*. New York: Holiday House, 1998.

Ford, Carin T. *Amelia Earhart: Meet the Pilot*. Berkeley Heights, N.J.: Enslow Publishers, Inc., 2002.

Jerome, Kate Boehm. *Who Was Amelia Earhart?* New York: Grosset & Dunlap, 2002.

Mara, Wil. *Amelia Earhart*. New York: Children's Press, 2002.

Web Sites

Amelia Earhart Birthplace Museum
    <http://www.ameliaearhartmuseum.org>

Amelia Earhart
    <http://www.kshs.org/kids>
Click on "Famous Kansans," then on "E" for "Earhart."

Index